Images of
Dunoon
and the Cowal Peninsula

Images of
DUNOON
and the Cowal Peninsula

Scoular Anderson

Argyll
publishing

First published 1998
Argyll Publishing
Glendaruel
Argyll PA22 3AE

British Library Cataloguing-in-Publication Data.
A catalogue record for this book is available from the British Library.

ISBN 1 874640 98 X hardback
ISBN 1 874640 93 9 paperback

Origination
Cordfall Ltd, Glasgow

Printing
Colour Books Ltd, Dublin

To my parents

Foreword

It was at the age of three months when a drunken landlady turfed me and my parents out of her Strone B&B that I first discovered Ardentinny. In those days it was as perfect a seaside village as could be found, and even though I went to school in London, I've always told myself that I grew up in that pearl perched on the crystalline edges of Loch Long.

Much has changed since then but my family has remained bound to the Cowal Peninsula with hoops of steel. My parents bought a cottage in Ardentinny, my grandparents moved from Glasgow into the Manse, where they gathered mussels (bed now, alas, defunct) grew raspberries and blew raspberries at their enchanted grandchildren.

My uncle opened the Primrose Tearooms specialising some thirty years before anyone else in Danish furnishings, Charles Schultz and boasting the best scones this side of Bannockburn.

One of my childhood joys was meeting the author of this gorgeous book, who once caught me stealing an After Eight from his mother's kitchen in Hunter's Quay and never told on me. Plus, he could draw, which instantly trebled his heroism.

Dunoon and Cowal is full of the deepest beauty and mystery. Each loch has its own personality, each area its peculiar charm. The Polaris has gone. The air is like wine. The red squirrels are returning to the Massan. My definition of happiness is to consume a pint of eighty shilling and a haddock and egg pie whilst watching the dusk deepening in the mirror of Loch Eck.

Emma Thompson

Emma Thompson

Contents

Preface

There are a number of books about Dunoon and the Cowal Peninsula. There are guides on archaeology, on history and on geology. There are guides on walks, cycling, where to go, what to see and when you've done all that, where to get the next ferry home. Is there room for another?

There are remarkable variations in the character of the Cowal Peninsula – from the grand and sombre, mist-draped highland scenery of the north to the island-dotted bays of the south and from the populated sea-side east to the remote and tranquil west. The fact that most people come by ferry gives the added excitement and expectancy of arriving at somewhere different.

I have enjoyed travelling around this area I know so well and looking at it afresh, picking out the images that seem to represent its many different faces.

This, then, is a souvenir in the best sense of the word and a somewhat personal one. I hope that travellers will occasionally open it to remind themselves of happy times in a beautiful place and that those already familiar with Dunoon and Cowal will enjoy this little record of its many faces.

Scoular Anderson
Hunter's Quay
February 1998

EIDERS are Britain's second most abundant duck and most of the population is in Scotland. The female plumage is a speckled brown while the males sport a striking pattern of black and white. The female lines her nest with feathers plucked from her breast which is collected to stuff quilts – hence the name eiderdown.

Every stretch of the Cowal coast has its resident group of Eiders and in winter these flocks can number a hundred or more giving their distictive mewing call.

THE COWAL PENINSULA is part of Argyll and Bute, a county with a ragged coastline, scattered with islands and cut by sea-lochs. Unravelled and stretched out, the coastline of Argyll would be longer than that of France.

The area of Cowal has been inhabited since ancient times as standing stones prove but it was the fashion for holidays by the sea in the nineteenth century that made the Cowal peninsula and its principal town, Dunoon, a popular place to visit.

The name Cowal is thought to come from *Comghall*, one of the Irish chieftains who ruled Argyll (then known as the kingdom of Dalriada) in the sixth century.

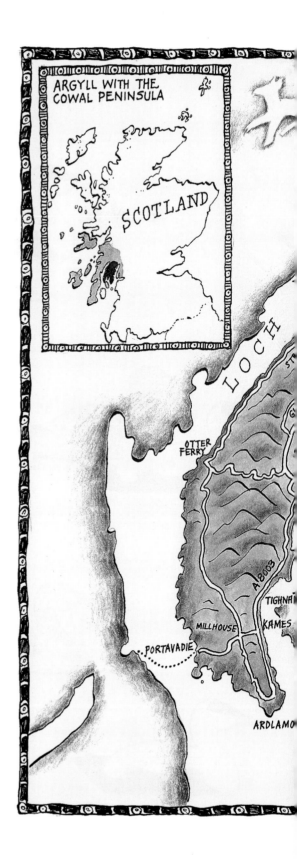

ARGYLL WITH THE COWAL PENINSULA

SCOTLAND

LOCH

OTTER FERRY

A8003

TIGHNA

MILLHOUSE

KAMES

PORTAVADIE

ARDLAMO

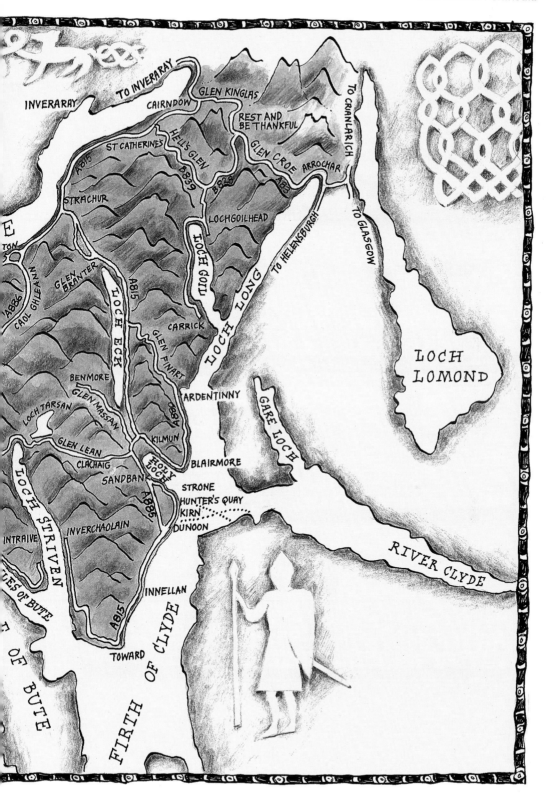

INVERARAY

TO INVERARAY

CAIRNDOW

GLEN KINGLAS

REST AND
BE THANKFUL

TO CRANLARICH

ST CATHERINES

HELLS GLEN

GLEN CROE

ARROCHAR

A815

B839

B828

A83

STRACHUR

LOCHGOILHEAD

TO HELENSBURGH

LOCH GOIL

LOCH LONG

TO GLASGOW

TON

GLEN BRANTER

LOCH ECK

A815

CARRICK

LOCH LOMOND

A986

CAOL GHLEANN

GLEN FINART

A880

BENMORE

GLEN MASSAN

ARDENTINNY

GARE LOCH

LOCH TARSAN

KILMUN

GLEN LEAN

CLACHAIG

HOLY LOCH

BLAIRMORE

SANDBANK

STRONE

HUNTER'S QUAY

A885

KIRN

DUNOON

INTRAIVE

LOCH STRIVEN

INVERCHAOLAIN

RIVER CLYDE

ES OF BUTE

INNELLAN

A815

FIRTH OF CLYDE

TOWARD

T OF BUTE

13

Perhaps one of the unique aspects of the nineteenth century was the large number of pleasure boats that sailed the River Clyde, the Firth and beyond. The very nature of the land meant that sea-travel was the easiest option. Fleets of paddle-steamers vied with each other to carry holiday-makers and day-trippers *doon the watter* from Glasgow to the resorts and distant lochs. At the end of the century there were over forty of such boats in service.

There is one reminder of these days – the paddle-steamer *Waverley*, built in 1947 and still plying the Clyde as a pleasure-steamer during the summer months. She is operated by the Paddle Steamer Preservation Society.

Fine liveries and grand names –
(left, from the top) steamers belonging to the North British Railway Company, The Caledonian Steam Packet Company, Buchanan's Steamers and The John Williamson and Turbine Syndicate.

(below) the Paddle Steamer *Waverley*

Dunoon

THE NAME DUNOON has had over forty different spellings in its lifetime. There is no doubt what the first part of the name means: *Dun* – a hill, usually a fortified one.

The second part is more problematic and some of the suggestions are: Hill of the Stranger, the New Fort, the Hill of the Ash Tree, the Hill of Foam and even the House of the Virgins (there was reputed to have been a nunnery nearby).

However, Fort on the River seems to be the accepted translation.

the statue of Burn's 'Highland Mary', now a famous Dunoon landmark, stands on Castle Hill

The fort or castle referred to no longer exists but the grassy hill to the south of the town is where it sat and it must have been an impressive sight. The Castle Hill itself was formed by molten volcanic rock 290 million years ago.

The castle had a good pedigree. During his reign, at the beginning of the twelfth century, King David I of Scotland made a Norman nobleman, Walter Fitzallen, his High Steward in charge of the royal household. This was the highest office in the land and by marrying into the clan of the Lamonts of Cowal, he became owner of Dunoon Castle. The office of High Steward eventually became hereditary and the family adopted the name Steward – or Stewart. Thus, when a Stewart became king of Scotland in 1371, Dunoon Castle became royal property.

In 1472 James III appointed to the post of Keeper of Dunoon Castle, Sir Colin Campbell, Earl of Argyll. He was requested to present the king with one red rose, annually, on the Feast of John the Baptist. This strange type of rent was called *blenche-ferme* and it meant the lessee rendered only a small token in acknowledgement of his lord's superiority. Other similar strange rents have included annual blasts on a hunting-horn and items of clothing (see Kilmun Church).

In 1573, Mary Queen of Scots stayed at the castle during a royal progress through her realm and the castle was used as a residence until the end of the seventeenth century. When Inveraray Castle became the official home of the Argyll family, Dunoon Castle fell into disrepair, its stones being pilfered for other building purposes.

The statue on the flank of Castle Hill commemorates Highland Mary, one of Robert Burns's many lovers. She was born in Dunoon but met Burns when she was in the employment of Burns's landlord. Burns called her Highland Mary because she spoke Gaelic and she and Burns married one another in the old custom of exchanging bibles across a stream. Mary died three years later. The statue was unveiled in 1896 and shows Mary looking wistfully towards Ayrshire, Burns's birthplace.

Castle House was built by the Glasgow merchant James Ewing and still stands on Castle Hill

The building that has pretentions of being a castle, sitting in what is now called Castle Gardens was built as a private house.

In 1822, James Ewing, wealthy businessman and MP for Glasgow, bought the ground around the Castle Hill and decided to build himself a marine villa on the site. The house was designed by the Glasgow architect David Hamilton who was one of the finalists in the competition for a design for the new House of Parliament at Westminster.

At that time, Dunoon was just a cluster of thatched cottages around the church and manse but Mr Ewing and his marine villa were going to raise the profile of Dunoon and start the fashion for holiday homes by the sea. There followed an explosion of building work and houses began to spring up all along the Clyde Coast. Very soon Dunoon became the most fashionable holiday resort in the West of Scotland.

In 1868 Dunoon became a parliamentary burgh and Ewing's Castle House and grounds were eventually bought by the town council in 1892. The house was used as town council chambers and a library but now is the home of Dunoon Heritage Centre which displays the town's history.

(Opposite and right) There are subtle differences in the styles of architecture to be seen in the houses of Dunoon and surrounding villages but all share the same Victorian heritage. Seaside towns tend to have a lopsided look as houses and windows crane for a glimpse of the sea.

The most unusual building in Dunoon is the pier. The first pier was built in 1835. Before that, passengers and luggage had to be ferried from steamer to shore in a small rowing boat. Traffic increased so much that the pier had to be replaced by a better structure in 1867. By the end of the century it was decided that two berths were needed and so an enlarged and improved pier was officially opened in 1898. Today the pier, with its curious Tudor-Chinese style, looks much as it did a hundred years ago.

A few hundred metres along the prom to the north stands the coal pier, now encorporated into a car-park. It was here that Puffers were beached on the sand to off-load their cargo of coal. The weighbridge for weighing the cartloads of unloaded coal has now been moved to the rear of the disused weighbridge house.

For many years, a picturesque addition to the pier was the three-masted schooner *De Wadden*, now in the Mersey Maritime Museum.

cod pier Dunoon

The Argyll Hotel was built at the beginning of the nineteenth century (now much enlarged) and sat on what was then the rocks of the beach. The sea was moved considerably further away with the construction of the promenade

The history of Dunoon can be traced in stone along the length of the main street.

The Parish Church (above) was built in 1816 but had to be enlarged several times to keep pace with the rising population – and the increased congregation during the summer months. The tower was raised eight feet to accomodate a clock and bell and give the church the suitably imposing air that the townsfolk then felt necessary. There was a church here long before the present one and it had a school attached to it. In the middle of the seventeenth century there is record . . . *Given yeirlie to ane schoolmaster wha sall remane at the kirk of Dunoon the saume of twa hundreth merks Scotis money.*

The town comissioners had to meet in hotels – and for a time, in the pier waiting room – before the burgh hall was built (below), in Scots baronial gothic, in 1874

Buildings for business followed the upsurge of house-building. Number 82 Argyll Street (above) was originally built as a bank, wearing relaxed country clothes

The Commercial Buildings, built in 1910, show touches of Art Nouveau

25

The high point in Dunoon's calendar is the Cowal Highland Gathering which takes place every year on the last Friday and Saturday in August.

The games had a modest beginning. On and off from 1871 athletic matches and games were held in the town. The first organised Highland games took place in 1894. Turn-out was poor so the Burgh Crier was sent through the town with his bell to announce that the entrance price had been reduced.

After the shaky start the Gathering continued to grow and has become reknowned for its pipe band competition. The first competition in 1906 attracted six bands. Nowadays, 150 or more bands is the norm – that's about 2,500 bandsmen.

Young dancers come from all over the world to take part in the Highland Dancing Competitions. Dancers are judged on their skills at the Sword Dance, Highland Fling, Reel and Seann Triubhas.

In one of the first Highland games, held at Invergarry in 1820, the prize of a fat sheep was offered to anyone who could twist the four legs off a cow. Thankfully, today's trials of strength are less messy. The heavy events include putting the ball and the hammer, throwing the weight and the most famous Highland games activity – tossing the caber.

Intense concentration as the judges listen to an entrant in the solo piping competition. Soloists play for fifteen to twenty minutes, the programme including a Pibroch (a theme and variations) as well as marches, strathspeys and reels. Careful note will be taken of fingering technique and interpretation.

More intense concentration as members of a pipe band tune up. In the band competitions points are awarded for piping, drumming and ensemble. The drum majors have their own competition.

It's not just the activities on the field that attract spectators. A fringe of stalls provides entertainments and things to buy from sporrans to funny masks. It's also time to catch up with old acquaintances.

CLOCH LIGHTHOU

GOUROCK

UPRIVER TO GLASGOW

KILCREGGAN

ROSNEATH PENINSULA

NORTH

MOUNTAINS ON WEST SIDE OF LOCH LOMOND

Travelling from Dunoon north along the prom you come to the boundary between Dunoon and Kirn (marked by signs attached to a lamp post). This is a good place to stop and get your bearings and enjoy the broad, spacious sweep of the Firth of Clyde. If you are lucky and the air is clear (only a handful of days every year) you will see Ailsa Craig – a great granite stack, the remains of an extinct volcano – fifty miles (eighty kms.) away to the south.

The yellow navigation beacons have been adopted by cormorants as ideal perches.

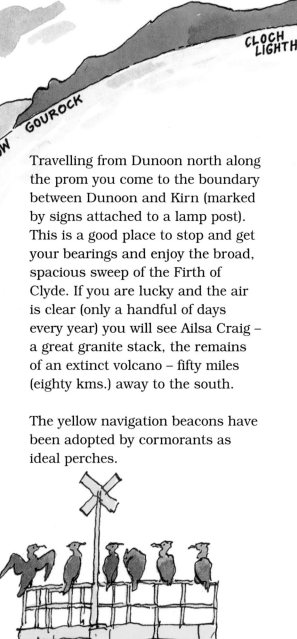

The beach that runs along beside the prom between Kirn and Hunter's Quay may not look very promising but its beautiful rocks make up for the lack of sand. They lie in ridges pointing out into the Firth, in many subtle shades of blue and green, sparkling with mica and banded with quartz.

Many of the boulders on the beach were deposited by moving ice during the ice age. The biggest one even has a name, *Jim Crow*, and is painted with eyes and a beak.

INVERKIP POWER STATION

AYRSHIRE COAST

ISLE OF CUMBRAE

GANTOCKS LIGHT

SOUTH

FIRTH OF CLYDE TO IRISH SEA

AILSA CRAIG

HOLY ISLAND

ISLE OF BUTE

COWAL COAST

DUNOON PIER

JIM CROW

Kirn

AT THE VILLAGE of Kirn there was once a pier but the pier and its buildings were sadly demolished long ago, They had unusual, yellow onion domes on the roof and there was a large clock which kept the village running on time.

Kirn is a relatively new name, not heard before the nineteenth century. It could simply be a corruption of the word cairn – or perhaps it referred to the quarry that lay nearby. An older name for the area is Ardenslate meaning promontory or height of the willows. Apparently the area was a well-known source of material for basket-making.

Behind the shops there once stood a pleasure ground for open-air concerts and dancing. Now you can stop off and play draughts or naughts-and-crosses in the promenade gardens. The Cowal Golf Course lies behind Kirn, up the brae by the church. It must be one of the best courses in the country for spectacular views.

Dionysus and Bacchus, gods of wine and revelry stand guard on either side of a bar door while other curious people sprout from a nearby building

Until the eighteenth century the upper reaches of the Clyde were shallow and not navigable but after a deep channel was dredged in the river, the city of Glasgow became a port and a centre of ship-building excellence. Those days have long gone but the river still teems with traffic of all kinds and it's impossible not to stop, lean on the prom railings and watch a boat go by.

Hunter's Quay

HUNTER'S QUAY once had an important connection with boats – in this case, the racing kind. The Quay takes its name from Mr Hunter of Hafton, a wealthy merchant who owned extensive lands on this part of the coast. The original name of this was *Camasreinach*, the Bay of Ferns.

In 1816 he commissioned a house from the architect David Hamilton – who also designed Castle House in Dunoon and Castle Toward. The Jacobean style house is now a hotel and the grounds are part of Hunter's Quay Holiday Village.

Hunter's Quay pier was built in 1828 and is one of the last few Clyde piers – out of over sixty – still in service. It is used by Western Ferries as their Cowal terminus.

Mr Hunter also built the hotel opposite the pier, now known as the Royal Marine Hotel. At the end of the nineteenth century the hotel was bought by the Royal Clyde Yacht Club for their headquarters. Hunter's Quay became one of the important yachting centres in the country and during Clyde Fortnight this part of the Clyde would be teeming with boats. High society came, too, including the Prince of Wales, later Edward VII, and a telegraph office was built so that important people could keep in touch with the outside world. This little building is now the Hunter's Quay post office.

Hunter's Quay sits at the mouth of the short Holy Loch and the road now winds its way along the west side. The Loch is perhaps so called because of the early church established at Kilmun but it was once known as *An Loch Seanta*, the charmed or magical loch. The land juts out into the loch at Lazaretto Point, marked by the tall tower of the war memorial. Lazaretto is the word for a quarantine station – from the biblical Lazarus, a leper – but in this instance the station was for possibly infected goods. It was built in 1807 but the government found that it was hindering trade and so the station was abandoned in 1840. All that remains is a small tower set on a ridge beyond the point.

Yacht races were still occasionally started from Hunter's Quay until fairly recently. Sometimes a make-shift starting place was organized on the beach or the prom and passers-by might be asked to help out with the raising of flags.

(Overleaf)
Holy Loch at
Lazaretto Point

Sandbank

THE VILLAGE of Sandbank has always been a place of industry. It once had a cooperage, a distillery and a printing works. More importantly, it was well-known as a yacht-building and maintenance centre. Two large yacht-yards once dominated the village, Robertson's and Morris & Lorimer's, neither now in existence. Robertson's, founded in the ninteenth century, built two of the America's Cup challengers, the *Sceptre* in the 1950s and the *Sovreign* in the 1960s. It also built and serviced RNLI lifeboats.

The village takes its name from the sandbank – or mudflats – at the top of the loch where boats were beached to receive cargo from the nearby gunpowder mills.

To the left of the inland road from Dunoon, up on the slopes behind Sandbank lie the archaelogical sites of Ardnadam Glen, with remains of Bronze and Iron-age settlements. To the right, the road continues along the loch-side.

The head of the Holy Loch is shallow and at low tide extensive mudflats are exposed providing feeding grounds for waders and other seabirds.

The housing development on the left as you leave Sandbank is a memory of the US navy. For more than twenty years their Polaris submarine base was located in the Holy Loch and the houses were built for navy personnel. Just beyond the houses, the large field sweeps up to a wooded knoll. This is *Tom nan Ragh* – Knoll of the Graves – an ancient Campbell burial place. This field is used regularly for sheepdog and motorbike trials.

The road next passes the Cot House Inn. The word Cot comes from *coite*, a punt or small boat used for ferrying passengers across the nearby River Eachaig.

During the Napoleonic Wars, Alexander Campbell of Ballochyle apparently used to drill a company of men here, known as the Kilmun Volunteers. They were ready to spring to the nation's assistance in event of an emergency. They almost did so when news reached them that the French Fleet had landed troops at Greenock. False information, needless to say.

Kilmun
Arboretum

JUST BEYOND Cot House the A880 road turns right down the east side of Holy Loch.

You are now within the boundaries of the Argyll Forest Park which covers more than 20,000 hectares. The idea of the park was conceived by the Forestry Commission in the 1930s and was created by the acquisition of a number of estates.

It contains not only large tracts of commercial forest but also mixed woodland, areas of planting for scientific study, some fine mountain scenery and a network of good walks.

One of the specialized areas is the Kilmun Arboretum, signposted where the River Echaig meets the Holy Loch. The Arboretum stretches up the warm, south-facing flank of Kilmun Hill and is planted up with tree species from around the world. Chinese Firs jostle with Australian Eucalyptus and the dark evergreen beeches of the southern hemisphere contrast with the brilliant autumn colour of specimens from North America.

There is a network of paths running through the Arboretum to suit every level of energy though the higher ones can be wet underfoot. Buzzards can often be spotted here and on a sunny day, if you walk carefully, you may see lizards basking on the grassy banks.

THE VILLAGES along the north and east of the Holy Loch sit in an an unbroken line along the shore. They are distinguished by their piers. The first village is Kilmun. There are scores of placenames beginning with *Kil* in Scotland. *Kil* – or *Cil* – means a monk's cell or place of worship and *Mun* was an early Christian saint.

St Mun built a church here in the seventh century. The collegiate church was founded in 1442 by Sir Duncan Campbell of Lochaw. The Campbells originally rented the lands from a kinswoman, the Countess of Mentieth, for the yearly payment of a pair of Paris gloves. The church was probably a *sang schule* with a company of singing boys – novices who attended the church for education and instruction.

The remains of the fifteenth century church tower stand beside the present church, built in 1841. Behind the church is the domed mausoleum of the Argyll family, which includes the body of the first Marquis of Argyll, beheaded after the English Civil War.

In the church yard you can see a *mortsafe* – a heavy iron grill which was laid over a grave to stop theft for medical disection. There are a good number of interesting gravestones in the churchyard – many with seafaring connections.

Kilmun Church

This is the burying Place Appointed for Daniel Taylor Ship-carpenter in Greenock and his Spouse and their Children 1758

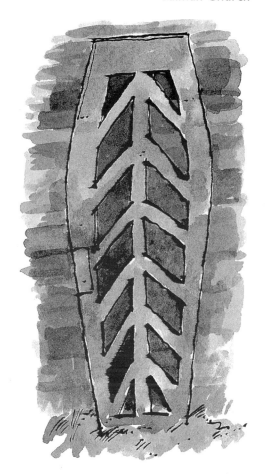

Bealach na Sreine – the Bridle Pass –
the site of this old drove road can be
seen from Cot House

Before modern coastal roads were
built, locals travelled from village to
village on the shortest route
possible, usually over the
mountains, keeping to the flanks of
hills well away from boggy land. If
you look across the top of the Holy
Loch from Cot House a smooth dip
in the hills, like a saddle, can be
seen. This is the *Bealach na Sreine*
– the Bridle Pass – and was the
route used by the inhabitants of
Inverchaolain on Loch Striven to
reach the outer world. It was also a

drove road, one of the many that once crossed Scotland, used by the crofters of the West to drive their herds to the markets at Crieff and Falkirk.

These cattle came in their thousands and in 1810 the inhabitants of Dunoon complained to the Commissioner of Highland Roads and Bridges about the lack of a good harbour to serve these herds and the resulting serious congestion and discomfort this caused.

The marine engineer David Napier built the pier and the hotel at Kilmun in 1827. He constructed a road to Loch Eck as a possible tourist route to the Western Highlands. Travellers would sail up the loch on a small steamer, catch a coach to Strachur, then another ferry across Loch Fyne to Inveraray, but the idea never really caught on.

After Kilmun comes Strone. The name is a corruption of the Gaelic word *sron*, a nose or promontory.

Strone has a small golf course perched precipitously on the brow of the hill. It also boasts one of those vitally useless bits of information: if you fly unswervingly straight as the proverbial crow due south from Strone Point, you don't touch land until you arrive at the coast of Spain.

At Strone the road rounds the point and runs north into Blairmore, named from the Gaelic 'Big Field'.

Another village, another pier. The little pierhouse at Blairmore has a Hansel and Gretel air about it with its sadly decayed gingerbreading.

At Blairmore there are several good examples of chuckie-stane gates – confections of white quartz often decorated with pebbles and sea-shells.

Blairmore pier building

(opposite) a yacht passes Strone Point

A chuckie-stane gate
at Blairmore

Loch Long

Long – a ship, the Ship Loch.
The Loch is mentioned in Icelandic
Sagas as Skipfjord, which means
much the same thing.

Ardentinny

THE ROAD becomes narrower and more exciting, eventually arriving at the village of Ardentinny. It's a peaceful little place which narrowly escaped becoming a depot for building deep-sea oil platforms in the 1970s. Unfortunately, the view across the loch is not as picturesque as it should be, the hillsides having been scarred by the development of the Royal Navy Armaments Base.

Ardentinny has a good beach of fine shingle – quite rare in this area. You can walk round the bay on the path that starts opposite the church. The path is flanked by silvery-leaved Sea Buckthorn bushes which are ablaze with

Ruins in Glenfinart near Ardentinny

orange berries in autumn. There is a carpark at the other side of the bay, which can be reached by a road situated a little way past the village and up the glen. From this carpark you can walk through adjoining woods – or all they way to Carrick Castle on Loch Goil if you have the stamina.

The name Ardentinny is from Gaelic *ard* – a promontory or height and *teine* – a fire. The fire could have been a signal – as a warning beacon or just to call the ferryman from the other side of the loch. It could also have been lit in some pagan religious ceremony.

Puck's Glen

Two glens worth visiting at the top of Holy Loch are Glen Massan and Puck's Glen.

PUCK'S GLEN was once part of the Benmore Estate. On a high promontory in the middle of the woods sat a little pavilion topped by a statue of Puck, the mythological figure of mischief. The building is now in the Younger Botanic Gardens. The Glen is more of a ravine through which a little river runs, tumbling down rocky chasms in waterfalls. It's well worth a visit. The path twists and turns, crossing and recrossing the river on bridges. There are huge mossy boulders and dripping rocks hanging with ferns – and icicles in winter. It has a rain-forest feel about it and you half expect to see a panther crouching on a fallen tree.

Glen Massan

GLEN MASSAN is a valley carved by glaciers. The scars and scratches made by moving ice can be seen on many rocks. At the narrow mouth of the glen the River Massan is biting into its bed and producing deep pools, waterfalls and sculpted rocks.

Glen Massan has associations with one of the ancient Celtic sagas *The Lay of Deirdre and the Children of Uisne*. Legend has it that Deirdre, known as Deirdre of the Sorrows, escaped from the kingdom of Ulster and took refuge in this glen. A manuscript relating the story was found here.

53

Benmore: the big mountain.
The mountain is one of the highest in the
area, but rather secretive as its summit is
mostly hidden by surrounding hills

54

Benmore

Benmore House, Younger Botanic Garden.
The garden boasts many spectacular trees
but it is for the Rhododendrons that people
come from all corners of the world

fountain with the clocktower behind

Giant Redwoods avenue planted in 1863

Botanic Gardens Benmore

AS THE NORTHBOUND A815 Glasgow road leaves the Holy Loch the hillsides and valley floor take on a park-like air. This was once part of the extensive Benmore estate which was owned in the nineteenth century by a succession of keen plantsmen. The remains of this estate are now encorporated into the Younger Botanic Garden which today is part of the Royal Botanic Garden in Edinburgh.

The first planting of the grounds around Benmore House began in the 1820s and the two rows of impressive Giant Redwoods were planted as an avenue leading to the house in 1863. James Duncan, a sugar refiner from Greenock, bought the estate in 1870 and erected many buildings in the grounds including the clock tower and a pair of large glasshouses which no longer exist. It was the Younger family, brewery-owners, who took over the estate in 1889 and added yet more decorative trees, shrubs and perennials. The grounds were eventually gifted to the nation in 1925. The house is now an outdoor education centre.

Loch Eck

THE GLASGOW ROAD continues northwards along the east side of Loch Eck. The stretch of water is modest compared to other Scottish lochs but it's a dramatically beautiful one. It is shallow and narrow and was once joined to the sea. A reminder of its ancient sea connections is the presence of a rare fish – the Powan – a freshwater herring, found only in one other place – Loch Lomond.

The surrounding mountains crowd in on the Loch creating dramatic views and strange, unpredictable winds. At the southern end Beinn Ruadh (the Red Mountain) and Clach Bheinn (the Stony Mountain) are streaked with the white of waterfalls during heavy spells of rain. The loch is now the water supply for Dunoon and area.

On the north flank of Clach Bheinn stands a curious outcrop of rock. Known locally as the praying monk and viewed from the right spot it's easy to see how the rock got its name. On the map it's called *poit dubh* – the black pot, or small still – and it looks just like the small whisky still once used by crofters albeit lying at a slightly drunken angle.

the praying monk

Coylet Inn on Loch Eck

Popular with fishermen, Lock Eck shows evidence of once being a sea loch. It is the habitat of the now rare Powan (below), a freshwater herring

59

Loch Eck with rainclouds

The meaning of the name Loch Eck is Horse Loch. The connection between the loch and horses is not clear. Perhaps it was the home of one of Scotland's mythical creatures – the Kelpie – who could take on many forms including the Water Horse, a dim and unpleasant creature. Fishing lines bated with dog carcasses placed on anchors rather than hooks were a suggested means of catching them. If you could get near enough to remove their bridles – and only women could do this – they became docile. However, as they could take on human form, the whole relationship with Water Horses becomes tricky.

Another curious name is that given to the almost submerged island at Dornoch picnic site – *Eilean a Chocaire*, the cook's island. It's possible than this island may have been a *crannog* – a type of iron-age dwelling on stilts. Perhaps the occupants were chefs!

(opposite) a hanging valley carved out by glaciers, high above the floor of the main glen in which Loch Eck sits

Glenbranter

JUST BEYOND the north end of Loch Eck a memorial stone stands on a knoll by the side of the road. Sir Harry Lauder the music hall entertainer once owned the local estate of Glenbranter and when his son was killed in the First World War, he erected this monument in his memory. The tragic event also inspired him to write one of his most well-known songs, *Keep Right On to the End of the Road.*

Lauder himself is commemorated in the Lauder Walks, a series of paths situated in the woodland across the glen. There is a carpark beyond Glenbranter village and the Forestry Depot. The paths meander through broadleaved woodland and lead to a gorge with waterfalls.

In the 1920s the Royal Botanic Garden in Edinburgh chose this site to plant a collection of Rhododendrons brought as specimens and seeds from an expedition to China. The plants needed damper, milder conditions than were available on the east coast of Scotland. The plants are still there and many have seeded themselves on the steep banks of the gorge.

Rhododendrons May '97

Strachur

STRACHUR is a village that seems to spread itself in all directions around a bay on Loch Fyne The original centre of the village is no longer on the main road. Follow the signs that say *Clachan* – Gaelic for village, or gathering of crofts – and you will find yourself at the old parish church.

It's an ancient site with a round graveyard though the church itself dates from 1789. There are medieval gravestones set into the church walls and bird-cage belfry.

The name Strachur is thought to come from the words *strath*, a valley and *corra*, a heron. And herons can be seen standing at the edge of Loch Fyne where the village spreads itself out along the shore.

A harbour was built here in front of the eighteenth century Strachur House. Near the post office and shop you can see a pair of entwined rowan trees. Rowan trees were often planted on either side of a croft door because it was believed they kept bad luck and witches at bay.

Pieces of the wood were incorporated into everyday objects – from butter churns to boats – by way of providing protection. Disastrous results would follow the cutting down of a rowan so when the road through Strachur was widened, the pair of entwined trees were carefully dug up and moved.

a heron stands stalking its prey at Strachur

The pair of entwined rowan trees at Strachur

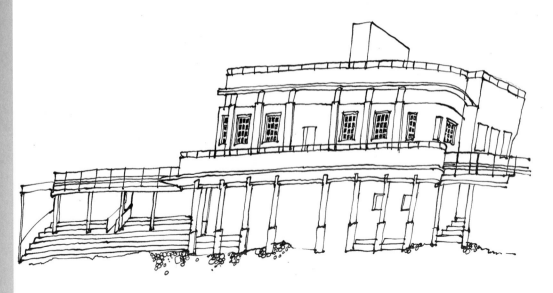

the Bathing Lido which once graced Dunoon's West Bay

the Cloch Lighthouse, Inverclyde coast

the Gantocks

West Bay

Travelling south from Dunoon (A815) you pass a paddling pool and swing park as you leave the town. To the right, the West Bay sweeps round in a gentle curve. There was a time when the bay was lined with the little huts of boat-hirers and their boats, with either engines or oars, lay on the shingle in gleaming, varnished rows.

At the southern end of the bay there once stood the Bathing Lido, built in the 1930s in the fashionable Art Deco style, with changing rooms and a tea-room. The site was an exposed and gravelly one and the lido fell out of favour with bathers and was eventually demolished.

In the times when swimmers were hardier than today, there were regular races between Dunoon pier and the Gantocks rocks and between Dunoon and the Cloch lighthouse.

The Cloch lighthouse on the other side of the river takes its name from the Gaelic *clach*, a stone. The lighthouse is two hundred years old and the first keeper was allowed to pilot ships on the river as long as he didn't neglect his principal duties. He was also under instructions not to sell spirits on the premises probably because the ferrymen of old were used to acting as barmen and dishing out whisky to their customers.The Gantocks light marks a treacherous shoal of rocks in midriver. Gantocks possibly comes from the Gaelic *caointeach* – a noisy and mischievous water sprite.

the family of geese

A handful of geese took up residence in the bay several years ago and now sport an extended family.

Before you leave the town on the road south,
Morag's Fairy Glen is worth exploring. The
entrance is through a little gate at the southern
end of the West Bay. The glen was once part of
the policies of Glenmorag House and there is a
pleasant walk up through the trees beside the
cascading Berry Burn to the folly at the top.

The area just south of Dunoon is known as the
Bullwood and here you will pass the Bullwood
quarry which provided building stone for
Dunoon. The rock is a schist called Greywacke
and the great tilted slabs give an impressive idea
of the structure of the land under the thin film of
soil and greenery.

If you keep an eye on the shore as you travel
southwards out of Innellan you will notice a
change in the character of the rocks, with red
sandstone making an appearance. This part of
Cowal lies along the Highland Boundary Fault
which runs across Scotland from Stonehaven in
the northeast to Bute in the southwest. This huge
crack was created many millions of years ago
and separates the northern mass of
Highland mountains from the sunken
Central Lowlands.

(opposite) Morag's Fairy
Glen

(right) The two types of
rock, sandstone and schist,
on either side of the
Highland Boundary Fault at
Innellan

Innellan Pier building

Innellan

INNELLAN PIER may not have been as picturesque as some others but it did boast a waiting-room. Like most other Clyde piers, it had a small tower with three disks. Such was the competition among the steamer companies, there was often a race for the pier between two or three vessels. To avert accidents, the piermaster would indicate which boat he wished to berth first – inside, middle or outside boat – by changing one of the black disks to white.

the remains of Knockamillie Castle

The village of Innellan once had its pier and its grand hotel – The Royal, which was destroyed by fire. If you take the winding road up the hill by the post office you come to Innellan Golf Course, perched precipitously on the flank of the hill. Nearby, there are the remains of Knockamillie Castle. It belonged to the Campbells of Auchnabreac and dates from the end of the sixteenth century. There isn't much to see of the castle but there is a good view of the Firth of Clyde below.

As you pass out of Innellan and the houses give way to farmland you can see a good example of a raised beach. About 8,000 years ago the sea covered these fields and the tree-covered ridge behind them was once a sea-cliff.

Toward Point once had a pier, too, but it is an exposed and windy place and there was an infrequent steamer service. The lighthouse was built in 1811. The little church-like building standing on the rocky shore once housed the foghorn machinery but is now a private residence.

Toward lighthouse

From the carpark just beyond Toward school there is a good view of the opening of the Firth of Clyde with the Ayrshire coast and Cumbrae island on the left and the Isles of Bute and Arran on the right. Behind you, the remains of a castle can be seen sticking out above the trees. This is Toward Castle which was once the principal seat of Clan Lamont. The earliest part of the castle, the tower, was built in the fifteenth century. During the next two centuries, other buildings were added round a courtyard. The Hall and the kitchen, with the remains of its huge fireplace can be seen to the left of the rear gatehouse. The castle was visited by Mary Queen of Scots in 1563 but less than a hundred years later it was in ruins. It was attacked by the Campbells of Ardkinglas in 1646, the inhabitants were massacred and the castle set on fire. Toward Castle is not to be confused with Castle Toward.

sea asters on a
Toward beach

(opposite) Toward Castle
(below) the remains of
the large kitchen fireplace

75

grotesque faces at the Castle Toward gatehouse

CASTLE TOWARD is a great crenelated mansion commissioned by the wealthy Glasgow businessman, Kirkman Finlay, who later became a provost of the city. The house was built in 1818 and the architect was David Hamilton (architect of Castle House and Hafton). Kirkman Finlay spent the next twenty years planting about five million trees on his extensive estate.

The imposing gatehouse looks like a castle in its own right. The stone wall now encorporated into the Toward Sailing Club enclosure was once part of a building which housed Castle Toward's swimming pool. It was glass-roofed and filled with heated seawater. Today Castle Toward is an outdoor education centre.

Toward Quay

Inverchaolain

Inverchaolain Church

AFTER TOWARD the road sweeps inland around one of the few pieces of good farmland in Cowal. And an area rich in Bronze Age burial sites. It passes the eighteenth century Knockdow House and arrives back at the coast, this time at the mouth of Loch Striven.

The road eventually comes to a dead-end but before that it passes the NATO refuelling base and Inverchaolain Church. The present church dates only from 1912, but the site is an ancient one and there was probably a church here in the thirteenth century. There are many interesting stones in the graveyard including one topped by an energetic yacht.

At the road-end, there is a footpath which continues up the loch-side. It a pleasant walk but can be very wet underfoot for the first few hundred metres.

Knockdow House

gravestone, Inverchaolain

Clachaig
Loch Tarsan
Loch Striven

JUST BEYOND Sandbank the B836 heads west. At the entrance to Glen Lean – the Broad Glen – there is a cluster of whitewashed cottages. The village of Clachaig once housed the employees of the gunpowder factory nearby. The rather grander factory manager's house sits on the opposite side of the road. All that remains of the once extensive works are crumbling walls. The business was started in 1843, reached its peak during the Crimean War and closed in 1903. The remote spot was chosen for safety reasons as well as the water-power needed to turn the millstones. Double walls were constructed on some of the buildings to reduce blast in case of an accidental explosion and flat roofs held water to douse the dangerous contents.

The powder was taken to Sandbank in barrels to be loaded onto boats

pulled up on the mud at the top of the Holy Loch. Many employees used to walk daily to the mills from Dunoon.

The evocative bleakness of Glen Lean is fast disappearing under conifer plantations but you will often see buzzards here, perched on the telephone poles. At the west end of the glen you pass Loch Tarsan, a man-made loch used for generating hydro-electricity. The name has no connections with the man who swung through the jungle trees but comes from the Gaelic *tarsuinn*, meaning across or oblique and in this case referring to the now-submerged Glen Tarsan which runs at an angle to the main valley.

The road dips down to the top of the fijord-like Loch Striven then rises steeply again to run across moorland before descending once more to Loch Riddon.

81

Colintraive

AS LOCH RIDDON comes in sight, you come to a road junction. The road to the left leads to Colintraive. The name comes from the Gaelic *Caol an t-snaimh* which means the Narrows of the Swimming because at this narrow stretch of water cattle and horses were swum across from the island of Bute to Cowal. This is still a crossing place as a car ferry now plies this route.

Displayed on the wall of the village hall is a door lintel from the old smithy that used to stand on the same spot.

83

Loch Riddon

L OCH RIDDON is a shallow but picturesque loch. The Campbells had a castle on *Eilean Dearg*, the Red Island, which sits in the middle of the Loch. In 1685 the 9th Earl of Argyll got himself involved in a plot to have the Duke of Monmouth succeed Charles II. His forces occupied several west coast castles in what became known as Argyll's Rising. The Earl lost his cause and his head and the government sent the frigate *Kingfisher* to blow up various Campbell strongholds including the Eilean Dearg castle.

The Earl led an adventurous life, having been imprisoned a number of times. On one occasion his wife arranged his escape dressed as her maid, as a surprising number of other prisoners have done throughout history.

the 9th Earl of Argyll

85

Kyles

THE NEW ROAD to Tighnabruaich, cut high into the crumpled schist rock is one of the most scenic in Cowal. It gives this good bird's eye view of the Kyles of Bute far below and there are several parking places where you can stop and admire the scenery.

a Puffer, the typical cargo vessel of the West of Scotland

a view down Kyles of Bute to Holy Island

Tighnabruaich
'85

Tighnabruaich

A S THE ROAD descends to
Tighnabruaich there is another
panorama of islands. The island of
Bute now sits to your left with the
small island of Inchmarnock in the
middle of the channel. To the right,
in the distance, are the peaks of the
island of Arran and the whale-like
hump of Holy Island. St Molaise
made this island his retreat in the
sixth century and a monastery was
built there in the fourteenth. Now it
is a religious retreat of a different
kind as the island is owned by the
Samye Ling Buddhists.

Tighnabruaich is now a popular
yachting centre and has a busy
sailing school. From the village you
can walk northwards, past the pier
and the boat-yard, along the coast
with good views of the Kyles. Across
the water you might catch sight of
the Maids of Bute. These are two
rocks fancifully considered to look
like two women. Para Handy, the
famous character created by the
author Neil Munro and the skipper
of the puffer *The Vital Spark*,
claimed he had painted clothes on
the maids, for modesty's sake.

The name *Tighnabruaich* means
The House on the Hill.

Kames

(opposite) shinty at Kames
(above) an unusual arrangment of stones in the old pier at Kames

BETWEEN THE VILLAGES of Tighnabruaich and Kames lies the Kyles Athletic shinty pitch. Shinty is a game whose origins are lost in the mists of time. St Columba was said to be a keen shinty player and he it was who reputedly brought the game from Ireland to Scotland when he settled on Iona. The name shinty come from the Gaelic *sinteag* meaning a leap and there is plenty of leaping, shinty being an energetic game in which there are no restrictions on the height at which the stick (*caman*) can be used. The balls are made of cork and covered in leather.

Kames was the port which served the powder mills at Millhouse. It's quay was known as Powder Quay and there was also a saltpetre works in the village making one of the ingredients of gunpowder. The remains of the steamboat pier show an unusual arrangement of vertical stones.

Windows on the modest little art nouveau church at Kames

Ardlamont

THE ROAD SOUTH from Kames continues its way down to Ardlamont Point, the most southerly tip of the Cowal Peninsula. The Lamonts were the most important clan in Cowal until the Campbells started flexing their powerful muscles. Several brutal massacres ended the Lamont hold over these lands.

Ardlamont house was the residence of the chief of Clan Lamont after the destruction of the Lamont stronghold of Toward Castle in the seventeenth century. It continued to be owned by the Lamonts until 1893.

The road now returns northwards, through farmland with glimpses of Loch Fyne, to the crossroads at Millhouse.

Millhouse

MILLHOUSE was another Cowal centre for gunpowder-making. The factory here was in operation between 1839 and 1921. The millwheels were turned by water power but steampower was introduced in 1855. Many trees were coppiced in Cowal for the making of charcoal. Charcoal was a constituent in the making of gunpowder.

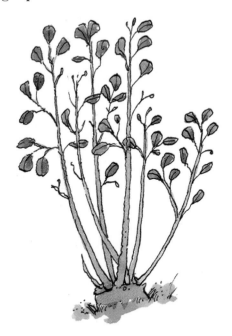

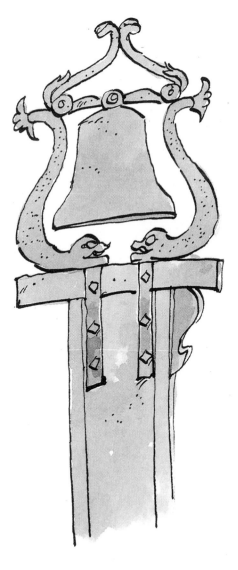

(above) a coppiced tree

(above) the factory bell still stands, supported by dolphins

(opposite) bullseye window on one of the former workers' houses, Millhouse

(above) Ascog Castle

(opposite) Stillaig standing stone, one of a pair which align with a hill on Knapdale thought to have formed a lunar observatory, was erected around 3000 years ago

Portavadie

AT MILLHOUSE CROSSROADS, one of the roads leads to Loch Fyne and Portavadie. The name Portavadie is made up of the Gaelic *port* – a harbour and *mhadaidh* – a dog, though a fox or wolf rather than the domestic kind. However, the second part of the word might come from *bhata* – a boat – the cove being a good anchorage. There may be some link between the name of the bay and the nearby Ascog Castle. The castle was a Lamont stronghold and it was the duty of the Lamonts of Ascog to man their chief's galley. Ascog is thought to mean The Bay of the Small Ship.

The castle was blown up by the Campbells at the same time as Toward Castle and never rebuilt. Their is evidence of a *crannog* (a lake-dwelling on stilts) on the loch and the castle may have had some connection with it. There is a public footpath which leads from Portavadie to Ascog Castle.

Natural woodland in Glenan Bay

Looking across Loch Fyne

Loch Meldalloch, popular for fishing

Portavadie was somewhat spoiled in the 1970s by the creation of an oil drilling platform construction yard and a village for the employees. The enterprise never took off, not a single platform was built and the village remained unused – a futile waste of money and desecration of the environment.

The bay is still worth visiting for the pleasant picnic area and the walk through the woods of ancient oaks and birch to Glenan Bay. There is now a fish farm at Portavadie and a car ferry which sails across Loch Fyne to Tarbert.

Back at the Millhouse crossroads, the northern route takes you past the reservoirs built to supply water to the gunpowder mills and known as the powder lochs. The bleak landscape of thin soil barely covering the rocky hills gives way to green farmland as you approach Kilfinan.

Kilfinan Hotel has operated as an inn on what was the main road to Tighnabruaich and Kames, from the mid-eighteenth century

Kilfinan church

Kilfinan

A grand tomb in the grounds of Kilfinan church

(right) An old drinking well on the way to Kilfinan

A CHURCH was first recorded at Kilfinan in 1253 and belonged to the Abbey of Paisley. The present church probably sits on earlier foundations and has been rebuilt several times.

Seen from the road above Otter Ferry,
a view of the Hebrides to the North West

Otter Ferry showing the sandspit or *oitir*

Otter Ferry

THE ROAD returns to Loch Fyne
yet again, dropping downhill to
the picturesque quay at Otter Ferry.
The name has nothing to do with
the animal but comes from the
Gaelic *oitir* meaning a sand spit and
a low tide the shingle bank can be
seen pointing out into the middle of
the loch for about a mile.

This was another ancient ferrying
place and the road that runs up the
hill behind Otter Ferry connected
Loch Fyne with the Clyde for those
jouneying west and east. This route
over the hill is known as
Ballochandrain, the pass of the

thorns, and from its summit on a
clear day you can enjoy a satisfying
panorama of some of the islands of
the Inner Hebrides. To the north
west the mountains of Mull can be
seen and directly opposite, the
islands of Jura and the hump-
backed Scarba. Between these two
islands lies the Gulf of
Corryvreckan and its famous
whirlpool which, in certain
weathers and at certain tides, can
been seen and heard from the
mainland nearby. The whirlpool is
named after Breacan, a prince of
Celtic legend.

the harbour at Otter Ferry

Loch Fyne & Strathlachlan

Strathlachlan churchyard

the village of Newton, built to house people cleared from the land to make way for sheep

FROM OTTER FERRY the road winds its way up the side of Loch Fyne, often clinging to the side of rocky outcrops. This is as remote as Cowal gets and in past times this area was the haunt of smugglers. It was known as The Kerry, from the Gaelic *ceamthramh* meaning a quarter portion of something, in this case, land. Tobacco, spirits and tea were brought to the remote bays of west Cowal where the smugglers had contacts. In 1750, for instance, the customs officers from Port Glasgow apprehended two ships off the

Cowal's west coa
Loch Fyne was a
for smugglers

Kerry coast, one laden with salt and the other with a cargo of barrels containing 60 gallons of rum and 54 gallons of brandy.

The road leaves the loch at Strathlachlan. The impressive ruins of Castle Lachlan lie on a promontory at the opposite side of Lachlan Bay. The three storey building dates from the fifteenth century though there is record of an earlier castle standing here at the beginning of the previous century.

A little further up the glen stands the Kilmorie Churchyard with the remains of a medieval chapel and further on still is the present Strathlachlan Parish Church built at the end of the eighteenth century.

The little village of Newton stands on the shores of Loch Fyne north of Strathlachlan. It was built to house crofters driven from their lands in the eighteenth century by the introduction of sheep.

Castle Lachlan

CASTLE LACHLAN, stonghold of
the Maclachlans. The name
comes from *Lochlann* the Gaelic
word for Norse invaders.

Medieval grave markings

Glendaruel

FROM LOCH FYNE and Newton, the A886 road swings round and south through the *Caol Ghleann* – the Narrow Glen, and into Glendaruel – the Glen of red blood. Legend has it that, after a battle between local clansmen and troublesome Vikings, the river in the glen ran red with the Norsemen's blood. On the other hand, it may just have been the peaty colouring of the water or some red sandstone deposits that gave rise to the name.

The Glen is looked down upon by the *Cailleach a Bheathrach* – the old woman of thunder. She takes the form of a large lump of stone high on the glen's western hills and was venerated by the local inhabitants –

much to the despair of a minister in the 1790s who shook his head at their superstitions. If any beasts went missing from the fields, it was assumed that the old woman had taken them and when displeased, she could send down floods from the hillside and ruin the crops.

Kilmodan Parish Church stands in the Clachan of Glendaruel. It was built in 1793 and there are three galleries inside, one each for the Campbells of Glendaruel, of Ormidale and of South Hall. There are medieval gravestones in the graveyard. It is thought that these stones were carved by intinerant stonemasons who copied the designs from pattern books.

Kilmodan Church, Glendaruel

One of many ruins of previous
settlements in Glendaruel

Views of deserted dwellings at the Glendaruel township of Kildalvin

In many places throughout Cowal you will find the sad remains of abandoned townships. The crofters who once lived in these ruined houses were turned off their farmsteads when landowners introduced sheep in huge numbers. In the middle of the eighteenth century the population of Glendaruel was a healthy eight hundred. Thirty years later it was less than half that.

The Glen bears the traces of many long-deserted dwellings – platforms on which stood turf-walled houses or mottes (wooden forerunners of the castle) as well as the remains of villages abandoned in the nineteenth century.

From the main road the field terraces of the long-abandoned township of Kildalvin can be seen across the glen on the western slopes. The ruins of many buildings are scattered across the hillside, including a kiln for drying grain. The remains of a burial ground and chapel stand near a healing well – the Christian and the pagan, side by side.

(right, clockwise from top left) Signs of settlement in Glendaruel:
a kiln house such as existed to dry grain in the township of Kildalvin;
an ancient ring-marked stone;
the gateway to the Glendaruel Estate, one of the great nineteenth century Highland land holdings;
a barn used for sheep and cattle feed

a view down Glendaruel

St Catherine's

FROM STRACHUR, the A815 road continues northwards along the shores of Loch Fyne. Stone was quarried at the village of St Catherine's and transported across the loch for the building of Inveraray Castle. A ferry plied across this route for centuries and the Middle Ages had their concessionary fares, too, as blind persons, priests and pilgrims were carried free.

The new town and castle of Inveraray were built by the third Duke of Argyll in the latter half of the eighteenth century. The Argyll family name is Campbell and it was the upwardly mobile Campbells that caused much hardship for

a ferry ran here for centuries across Loch Fyne from St Catherine's to Inveraray

other clans, including, on many occasions, the Lamonts of Cowal. Having said that, in their involvements with power, politics and intrigue, many noble Campbell heads rolled.

The town and castle at Inveraray with its bridges and parkland presents a pleasing view across the loch.

St Catherine's lays claim to having Britain's smallest Post Office

St Catherine was a native of Alexandria in Egypt. She was destined to be martyred on a spiked wheel but was beheaded instead. Perhaps the medieval chapel that once stood here was dedicated to her.

Hell's Glen in Autumn

Hell's Glen & Lochgoilhead

THE ROAD climbs steeply away from Loch Fyne and at its summit the B839 turns off toward Lochgoilhead down *Gleann Beag* – the small glen – more commonly known as Hell's Glen.

The word *goil* is assumed to be from the Gaelic for a fork, as the loch branches off the larger Loch Long. The loch is surrounded by high mountains and the area is very much a holiday centre for outdoor pursuits.

(left) The Church of the Three Holy Brethern at Lochgoilhead is medieval in origin

(opposite) Waterfall on the Lettermay Burn

Carrick Castle

AT THE SOUTHERN END of Loch Goil stands Carrick Castle. The tall tower was built in the late fourteenth century and was a Campbell stronghold. At one time it had a drawbridge spanning a deep ditch on the landward side. Mary Queen of Scots stayed here in 1563 and the castle was partially destroyed by government forces after Argyll's Rising in 1685. The building has been much added to and altered over the centuries and the present owner is restoring it as a residence.

Carrick Castle

Rest and Be Thankful

THE OTHER ROUTE from Loch Goilhead is the B828 Glen Mor Road which climbs to The Rest and Be Thankful, the 860ft (262m) summit of the pass between Loch Long and Loch Fyne.

Cowal has no official boundary at its joining point with the rest of Argyll but the main Glasgow-Inveraray road (A83) that passes here forms a convenient finishing point, running as it does across the top of the peninsula from Loch Long to Loch Fyne.

This was another ancient drove road linking the west with central Scotland and one eighteenth century traveller encountered herdsmen driving five thousand cattle to Falkirk market. Many famous feet have climbed this winding road, including Dr Johnson with his friend Boswell and the poets Keats and Wordsworth, all doing a grand tour.

The road was improved by General Wade and Major William Caulfeild,

(left) Ben Arthur, known as The Cobbler, at 881m is very popular with hillwalkers

(below) looking down Glen Croe from the Rest and be Thankful pass – one traveller saw this glen as the seat of melancholy where the sun's rays seldom penetrated
(opposite) Lochan Restil at the head of the pass

builders of many military roads across Scotland in the eighteenth century. Caulfeild put his engineering skills to domestic uses, too, by designing a cradle hoist in his house at Inverness for lifting inebriated guests to their bedrooms.

The old, road can be seen snaking its way laboriously up Glen Croe just below the present-day road. Its bustling traffic seems to soften the harsh descriptions of this glen made by visitors in previous times. ' One traveller saw it as 'the seat of melancholy seldom cheered by the rays of the sun.' Another said, 'Nature seems to have used her utmost efforts in collecting as much rock and as little verdure as possible.'

We are in Munro country which is the label given to the Scottish premier league mountains – those over 3,000 feet (914 metres). These were classified by Sir Hugh Munro in 1891 and Munro Bagging – climbing all 238 peaks – has become a popular activity.

(above) The gardens at Ardkinglas boast several of the highest trees in Britain

(opposite) A Loch Fyne fishing boat – at one time around 600 boats would work from Loch Fyne making Loch Fyne kippers (smoked herring) famous worldwide

Loch Fyne

FOR THE FINAL LEG of this journey round Cowal you must return to Loch Fyne down Glen Kinglas on the A83 Inveraray Road.

In the fresh, clean water of the head of Loch Fyne at Cairndow, lie commercial oyster beds. The business was started in 1978 and there is now a stock of about two million oysters in net bags, lying on metal stands along the seaweedy fringes of the loch. The oysters eventually disappear over the Rest and Be Thankful in vans, heading for various parts of the country – and for Glasgow airport, where they are dispatched to places as far away as Hong Kong.

This huge sea loch has long provided harvests. It was once famed for its herrings and no respectable breakfast was complete without a Loch Fyne Kipper. Thomas Thornton, writing at the beginning of the nineteenth century, told of around six hundred fishing boats at work on the loch and that between two hundred and three hundred horses arrived every day during the fishing season to carry barrels of fish to all parts of the country.

As has been seen at Benmore Gardens and Glenbranter, this part of Scotland has a climate which suits rhododendrons. More of these spectacular shrubs can be seen in Ardkinglas Woodland Garden, situated near the church at Cairndow. The gardens were established around 1875 and boast several record-breaking trees – including the tallest and broadest of certain species in Britain.

The handsome octagonal Kilmorich Parish Church at Cairndow was built in 1816. The original medieval church lay at the other side of Loch Fyne where a graveyard remains behind the Oyster Bar

Cairndow

THE POET WORDSWORTH and his sister stayed in the inn at Cairndow (the black cairn) on their travels through Scotland in 1803, accompanied by fellow poet, Samuel Taylor Coleridge. Dorothy Wordsworth kept a journal of their travels and for the adventure they bought a horse which was 'aged but stout and spirited'. The poor animal came near to a nervous breakdown after negotiating the capricious tracks and wild ferry-crossings of the West of Scotland. The trio travelled in a jaunting car which apparently caused much amazement and amusement among the local inhabitants.

Thankfully, travelling is easier nowadays and a good deal quicker – but the peacefulness of Cowal may persuade you to go at a gentler pace and you can enjoy many scenes that have changed little since the Wordsworths' time.

strange creatures around Cowal – did you see them?

For more information about
Dunoon and the Cowal Peninsula,
contact Argyll, the Isles, Loch
Lomond, Stirling & Trossachs
Tourist Board,
7 Alexandra Parade,
Dunoon,
Argyll PA23 8AB.
Tel 01369 703785

Other books by Argyll Publishing

Dunoon Pier
a celebration
Ian McCrorie
128pp 246 x 174mm
1 874640 68 8 £12.99 hbk
b&w and colour photos throughout
November 1997
foreword by Brian Wilson MP
In this centenary year of the building of the landmark of the Clyde estuary that is etched on the memory of millions, Dunoon Pier – a celebration is a timely book. Lavishly illustrated throughout, the pressure of river traffic to build the pier is recounted. Though the age of mass pleasure cruising may have declined, Dunoon pier is still an important terminal for commuter and motor traffic.

Ian McCrorie is a widely known River Clyde historian and writer.

"Ian McCrorie walks the planks with serene assurance."   William Hunter *The Herald*

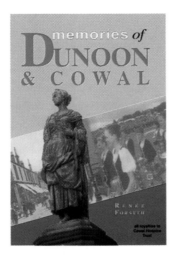

Memories of Dunoon & Cowal
Renée Forsyth
160pp 246 x 174mm pbk
illustrated
1 874640 28 9 £9.99
April 1997